TECH **TITANS**

AMAZON

BY SHANNON BAKER MOORE

CONTENT CONSULTANT

Anthony Rotolo
Media Scholar, Speaker, and Consultant

Essential Library

An Imprint of Abdo Publishing | abdobooks.com

ABDOBOOKS.COM

Published by Abdo Publishing, a division of ABDO, PO Box 398166, Minneapolis, Minnesota 55439. Copyright © 2019 by Abdo Consulting Group, Inc. International copyrights reserved in all countries. No part of this book may be reproduced in any form without written permission from the publisher. Essential Library™ is a trademark and logo of Abdo Publishing.

Printed in the United States of America, North Mankato, Minnesota.
082018
012019

Cover Photo: Elaine Thompson/AP Images
Interior Photos: Amy Harris/Invision/AP Images, 4–5; Rich Pedroncelli/AP Images, 7; Andy Rogers/AP Images, 9, 12–13, 19; Nikki Kahn/The Washington Post/Getty Images, 15; DW Labs Incorporated/Shutterstock Images, 22; Red Line Editorial, 25, 73, 96; Barry Sweet/AP Images, 26–27; Mark Lennihan/AP Images, 31, 41; Elaine Thompson/AP Images, 35, 61, 71, 85; Yuganov Konstantin/Shutterstock Images, 36–37; John Minchillo/AP Images, 43; Ted S. Warren/AP Images, 46–47; Scott Olson/ Getty Images News/Getty Images, 50; Shutterstock Images, 54; Mary Altaffer/AP Images, 56–57; Polaris/Newscom, 62–63; Robert Daemmrich Photography Inc/ Corbis/Getty Images, 67; David Paul Morris/Bloomberg/Getty Images, 69; Bess Adler/Bloomberg/Getty Images, 74–75; Lisa Werner/Moment Mobile/Getty Images, 80; Dean Bertoncelj/Shutterstock Images, 83; Chip Somodevilla/Getty Images, 88; Ralph Goldmann/picture-alliance/dpa/AP Images, 90–91; Phelan M. Ebenhack/AP Images, 94

Editor: Arnold Ringstad
Series Designer: Laura Polzin

Library of Congress Control Number: 2018948240

Publisher's Cataloging-in-Publication Data

Names: Baker Moore, Shannon, author.
Title: Amazon / by Shannon Baker Moore.
Description: Minneapolis, Minnesota : Abdo Publishing, 2019 | Series: Tech titans | Includes online resources and index.
Identifiers: ISBN 9781532116858 (lib. bdg.) | ISBN 9781532159695 (ebook)
Subjects: LCSH: Amazon.com (Firm)--Juvenile literature. | Online shopping--Juvenile literature. | Web retailing--Juvenile literature. | Technology--Juvenile literature.
Classification: DDC 381.45002028--dc23

CONTENTS

CHAPTER **ONE**

THE RICHEST MAN IN THE WORLD

On July 27, 2017, Jeff Bezos became the richest person in the world for a few hours. The 54-year-old Bezos is the founder and chief executive officer of the shopping website Amazon.com. On that morning, Amazon's stock price rose. Bezos's personal holdings of Amazon stock meant that his wealth rose, too, reaching $92.3 billion.[1]

But Bezos's ranking didn't last long. Just a few hours later, Amazon's stock price dipped, and Bezos was no longer the richest person in the world. Nevertheless, Amazon's stock price soon rose again and pushed Bezos back to the top spot, where he remained in early 2018. By March of that year, Bezos's fortune was estimated at approximately $127 billion.[2]

Despite his status as a billionaire businessman, Bezos often dresses casually in his public appearances.

This was more than the 2016 gross domestic product of the nation of Ecuador.

FROM BOOKS TO EVERYTHING

Amazon, the company that propelled its founder to such great riches, started out as a small online bookstore run out of Bezos's garage in Seattle, Washington. Since then, Amazon has grown into a company that has changed how Americans shop and what they expect from an online store. As one of the most famous shopping websites in the world, Amazon sells everything from cat food to kayaks to hissing cockroaches.

But Amazon is much more than a shopping website. Users can order groceries through Amazon Fresh, a grocery pickup and delivery service. They can buy and

Amazon is best known for its retail and logistics operations, but the company has branched out into many other related areas.

stream movies produced by Amazon or have DVDs delivered with two-day free shipping via Amazon Prime. If a customer is not home, the delivery person can use Amazon Key to unlock the door and leave packages inside his or her house. A person can order household products instantly using an Amazon Dash Button. And through Amazon Services, a user can hire a person to clean his or her house.

INNOVATION AND CHANGE

As Amazon's founder and leader, Bezos has pushed the company to innovate and change. Amazon now builds tech devices like the Kindle e-reader, the Fire tablet, and the Echo speaker, which features the voice-activated personal assistant Alexa. Amazon is experimenting with package delivery by drone. Bezos has used his Amazon profits to fund experimental space travel. He started the aerospace company Blue Origin in hopes of making space flight more affordable and available to the public.

Amazon has been innovative in other ways as well. In addition to selling products itself, the company lets other sellers use its website to advertise and sell products. One of the biggest moneymakers for Amazon is Amazon Web Services (AWS), Amazon's cloud service, created in 2002.

JEFF BEZOS

Jeff Bezos, the founder of Amazon, was born on January 12, 1964, in Albuquerque, New Mexico. Bezos was the son of Jackie Gise and Ted Jorgensen. But Bezos's mother divorced Jorgensen and remarried. Her new husband, Mike Bezos, legally adopted four-year-old Jeff. Bezos's mother was a stay-at-home mom. Mike was an engineer for oil company Exxon.

During his childhood, Bezos and his family moved several times, living in Houston, Texas, and Pensacola, Florida. Bezos often spent summers at his grandparents' ranch in Texas, where he worked with his grandfather doing chores and helping fix machinery. As a kid, Bezos was interested in science and inventions. He was a tinkerer who built a solar cooker from an umbrella and built a variety of alarms and traps to keep his younger siblings out of his room. Intelligent and hardworking, Bezos graduated at the top of his class from his Florida high school.

Bezos studied electrical engineering and computer science at Princeton University. After Bezos graduated in 1986, he eventually got a job in New York City working for an investment company called DESCO. Bezos excelled, and at 26 years old, he was the youngest vice president DESCO had ever had. In early 1994, Bezos's boss asked him to research possible internet business opportunities. Bezos discovered that use of the internet was growing quickly. He started to think about what kind of business would work well as an internet business.

In July 1994, Bezos and his wife MacKenzie left New York City and drove to Seattle, where they started Amazon. They had been married for one year. In 2018, Bezos lived near Seattle with MacKenzie and their four children.

Bezos has been the CEO of Amazon from the very beginning.

9

Organizations including Netflix, Pinterest, and even the US government use AWS to run their websites and streaming services. AWS provides more than 40 percent of all cloud computing services available online.[4]

THE RISE OF THE INTERNET

Today Amazon's phenomenal success is easy to see. But when Bezos first started Amazon in July 1994, many people weren't even sure what the internet was. It took almost one year to get the website up and running. When Amazon received its first online order on April 3, 1995, few people were using the internet, and even fewer were using it to shop. Many people predicted that Amazon would fail.

No one, not even Bezos, could have predicted the company's stunning success. Bezos was smart, an outstanding engineer and computer science student who had graduated from Princeton University, one of the top universities in the United States. He was also a hard worker. In fact, before Bezos started Amazon, he already had a good job as a vice president at an investment company in New York City. Bezos decided to leave his good job, move across the country to Seattle, and start a small online bookstore in his garage. He wanted to build his own business from the ground up, and he believed the internet was the way to do it.

Today, Amazon is a part of everyday life for millions of people worldwide. In the US, 40 cents of every dollar spent online is spent on Amazon.[5] The company has dramatically shaped not just the book business but even people's buying habits and online shopping in general. And if Bezos has his way, Amazon will continue to be a leader in the technology industry for years to come.

WHY SEATTLE?

Bezos knew what he wanted to sell online, but he had to decide where to base the new company. He chose Seattle for several reasons. Seattle was the home of the aerospace company Boeing, the software company Microsoft, and the University of Washington. This meant there were plenty of experts in computer science and technology who could work at Amazon. Seattle was also close to a large book distribution company, making it easier for Amazon to stock its primary products.

CHAPTER **TWO**

IT BEGAN
WITH BOOKS

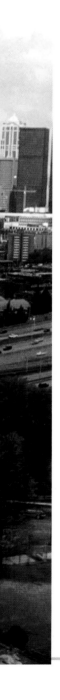

B ezos started Amazon as a bookstore, but he had bigger ambitions. With his engineering and computer science background, Bezos understood the emerging technology of the internet and its incredible potential. In early 1994, Bezos discovered the internet was growing more quickly than most people realized. Between January 1993 and January 1994, online activity had increased by approximately 230,000 percent. Bezos said, "I'd never seen or heard of anything that grew that fast."[1]

Bezos realized the internet was not just going to grow big—it was going to explode. He started to think about what kind of business would work well online. Bezos made a list of 20 possible products he could sell online. In the end, he decided on books. Books don't have an expiration date like food. A book from one store

Amazon's early days laid the foundation for the company's dramatic growth several years later.

FROM CADABRA TO AMAZON

Bezos wanted an online bookstore that offered millions of books. No brick-and-mortar bookstore could hold that many books. No book catalog could list that many books. But with the help of the internet, Bezos's online bookstore could be the biggest bookstore in the world. It was like magic. This might be why Bezos originally called his company Cadabra, as in "abracadabra." However, some people thought the name *Cadabra* sounded too much like the word *cadaver*, meaning a dead body. So in October 1994, Bezos opened up the dictionary to search for a new name. He settled on Amazon. It began with *A*, so it would appear at the beginning of alphabetical lists. The Amazon was also the world's largest river, a good name for a company aiming to become the world's largest bookstore.

is identical to the same book at another store. Books are easy to pack and ship. People don't need to try on books to see if the color or fit is right. Plus Bezos was a reader himself. He liked books and knew that people who liked to read also bought books as gifts for others.

Amazon started out in a Seattle garage. Besides Bezos and his wife MacKenzie, who worked as the office accountant, the company had one employee: Shel Kaphan, a computer programmer from California. One month later Paul Davis, a computer programmer from the University of Washington, was hired. According to Kaphan, when he started there were no computers, and they had no idea how to write computer code for a website. Bezos worked on learning about the book business while

SHEL KAPHAN

Shel Kaphan was Amazon's first employee and one of its two original programmers. Kaphan worked for Amazon from 1994 to 1999, and Bezos has called Kaphan "the most important person ever in the history of Amazon."[2] Bezos and Kaphan first met in 1994, before Bezos had started Amazon. A coworker introduced him to Kaphan, a computer programmer living in Santa Cruz, California. Bezos flew to California to persuade Kaphan to come to work on a new e-commerce site. Kaphan had a bachelor's degree in mathematics, and he had worked in both the book business and the computer industry.

In October 1994, Kaphan moved from California to Washington and became Amazon's first employee and main programmer. One month later, they hired a second programmer, Paul Davis. According to Kaphan, "When I first got there, we didn't have any computers yet, so the first job was to go shop for some computers and decide what database systems we were going to use and what software was available. I mean, nobody knew how to write Web sites at that point in time. I had never done it before. So, we had to figure out how [we] were going to do that."[3]

Approximately two and a half years after the company was founded, Bezos hired other technical managers. Kaphan's job was split among them, and he was made chief technology officer. But Kaphan felt Bezos had given him an ornamental position with no real authority or decision-making power. He preferred being a hands-on builder rather than a manager anyway. Kaphan says he felt the situation wasn't handled "in the right way."[4] Kaphan left Amazon in 1999.

Kaphan had been interested in the internet since its early days in the 1970s, but the introduction of the World Wide Web in the 1990s made it clear that incredible business opportunities were available online.

Kaphan and Davis focused on creating the website. Approximately six months later, in the spring of 1995, the test version of the website was ready for a trial run.

By today's standards, Amazon's first website looked clunky and unprofessional. But by the standards of the day, the website was impressive. It had a shopping cart, the ability to process secure credit card payments, and a basic search engine.

On July 16, 1995, Amazon's website opened for business. The first week it received $12,000 of book orders, shipping $846 worth of those orders. The second week it got $14,000 of orders and shipped $7,000 worth. By the end of the first month, Amazon had sold books to people in all 50 states and in 45 countries.[5] Every day the orders increased, and the fight to keep up with business got harder.

Bezos viewed Amazon as a tech company more than a bookstore. Books were a great place to start, but Bezos's goal was to become the "everything store."[6] Technology was the way to get there. From the beginning of Amazon, Bezos built his company upon a few key principles. They included cutting costs, experimenting and innovating, and focusing on long-term plans rather than short-term goals.

WORKING HARD

Bezos worked long hours, and he expected employees to do the same. Bezos argued that Amazon needed to grow quickly in order to compete with established retailers, such as Walmart. He also knew that with the growth of the internet, online shopping would become more and more competitive. At times, people felt like they were expected to work seven days a week. Susan Benson, a long-time employee at Amazon, said, "Nobody said you couldn't [take the weekend off], but nobody thought you would."[7]

CUSTOMER OBSESSION

Bezos believes if it's good for the customer, it's good for Amazon. Bezos calls this "starting with customers, [and] working backwards."[8] Bezos is "customer obsessed" and takes time to review customer emails and complaints sent to his public email address. Bezos has even checked the wait times for calls to customer service. During the 2000 holiday season, the time of year when Amazon was at its busiest, Bezos held a meeting with Amazon's company leadership. He asked one of the company vice presidents how long customers had to wait before their call was answered. Bill Price, the vice president in charge of customer service, said wait times were less than one minute. Bezos said, "Really? Let's see."[9]

He then called Amazon's customer service number. Everyone in the room—about 30 people—sat and waited as the seconds ticked by. Bezos got angrier and angrier. Four and a half minutes later, a customer service representative finally answered. Bezos slammed down the phone and started yelling at Price.

Another early employee, Christopher Smith, worked in the warehouse. He often arrived at 4:30 a.m. and stayed until after midnight. He usually biked to work, and he was gone so much that eventually his car, which was illegally parked outside his apartment, was towed away without him even noticing.

DOOR DESKS

When Bezos first started Amazon in his garage, he needed a couple of desks to put computers on. He went to a local home improvement store looking for some inexpensive desks. He quickly realized that doors were cheaper than desks. So he bought a door, attached some legs to it, and turned it into a desk. Today, door desks are still an important part of Amazon's culture, and thousands of employees use them. The door desk has become a symbol for one of Amazon's key values: frugality. And every year Amazon gives out "Door Desk Awards" to employees who come up with "well-built ideas that help deliver low prices to customers."[10]

CUTTING COSTS

From the beginning, Bezos pushed for lower costs for customers by cutting costs at the company. Tech companies are famous for offering their employees perks such as free meals, gym memberships, massage chairs, and extra paid time off. Amazon did not follow this trend. Bezos is famous for frugality. The company originally used inexpensive desks built from doors. Bezos also cut costs by making employees pay for their own parking. Although Bezos leases

Desks made of repurposed doors became a powerful symbol of Amazon's corporate frugality.

a private jet, Amazon doesn't have a company plane. Bezos requires top executives to fly on cheaper coach seats rather than flying first class.

Despite this frugal attitude, Bezos has been willing to spend money investing in Amazon and buying new companies and technologies that can help it grow. Amazon has spent—and often lost—hundreds of millions of dollars buying other internet companies and investing in technology.

INNOVATE AND EXPERIMENT

Throughout its history, Amazon has experimented with new products and features for online shopping. Some of Amazon's innovations seem commonplace today but were revolutionary back when online shopping was just beginning. Amazon pioneered online reviews, one-click payments, and the practice of listing new and used products side by side.

As an engineer, Bezos believes in invention and experimentation. According to Bezos, "We have had many failures. If you want to be inventive, you have to be willing to fail because you have to be willing to do experiments. And it's not an experiment if you know in advance it's going to work."[11] Bezos continues to innovate in order to keep Amazon successful.

COMPETITION

When Amazon began as an online bookseller in 1995, it was much smaller than its competitors, including national bookstore chains like Barnes & Noble and Borders. When Barnes & Noble first started its website in 1997, Amazon had just 150 employees. Barnes & Noble had 30,000.[12] Some business experts predicted that Amazon would soon be crushed by the established company.

Bezos knew Amazon had to grow fast in order to compete. Bezos needed more money to invest in Amazon and to grow his company. In May 1997, Amazon became a publicly traded company. A publicly traded company allows any member of the public to buy or sell the company's stock. Going public, known as an initial public offering (IPO), is a fast way for a company to raise money. Amazon quickly raised $54 million.[13]

Bezos says he's more focused on customers than competition, but he's fought ferociously to win in business. Just three years after it opened, Amazon moved into selling other products besides books, first with CDs and DVDs, then toys and electronics. Over the years, Amazon has bought out rival businesses or put them out of business by dropping prices so low that other

Barnes & Noble is the largest of Amazon's brick-and-mortar competitors.

companies can't compete. At times, Amazon has even sold products for less than the price it paid.

Amazon eventually grew to become the dominant bookstore, overtaking both Barnes & Noble and Borders.

Borders went out of business in 2011. In 2016, Barnes & Noble's revenue was approximately $4 billion.[14] Amazon's was approximately $136 billion.[15]

FOCUS ON THE LONG TERM

In the late 1990s, more and more internet companies were created. The internet seemed to be the next hot thing, and some people were making fortunes overnight with these new businesses. But these dreams evaporated around the year 2000. People realized the promise of the internet was not translating into real-world revenue for online companies. Internet-focused firms began losing funding, and many went out of business.

This crash seriously impacted Amazon. It had bought internet companies that ultimately failed. People started wondering if Amazon would also fail. Investors began selling Amazon stock. But Bezos was focused on the long term.

At a conference in 2001, Bezos held up two graphs. The first graph tracked Amazon's stock price from its highest price in 1999 ($107 a share) down to its lowest price in 2001 ($6 a share). But the second graph showed Amazon's stock price rising from its initial stock price of

$1.50 a share in 1997 to its current price at the time, $12 a share.[16] Bezos's point was that while the company wasn't doing as well as it had done in the past, compared to where it started out the company was doing great. It just depended on how you looked at it.

Unlike other tech companies such as Apple, Amazon is not a company that generates a lot of profit, despite its billions of dollars in revenue. That's because Bezos invests Amazon's income back into growing the business, spending money on better hardware and software, more employees, more fulfillment centers, and research and development of new technologies. Bezos claims most companies want short-term success that can be accomplished in two or three years. Amazon, on the other hand, is willing to wait for greater long-term gains.

AMAZON REVENUE AND PROFIT[17]

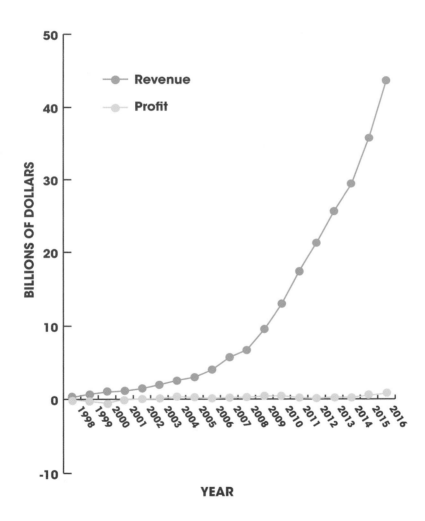

Amazon's revenues have been climbing significantly, but its profits have remained relatively low and consistent. Bezos prefers to drive the company's revenue into investing and growing its business.

CHAPTER **THREE**

CHANGING BOOKS AND MEDIA

A mazon's growth was explosive. The company took its first online order on April 3, 1995. By December 1996, it had 180,000 customers. By October 1997, it had more than one million customers. Sales grew from $15.7 million in 1996 to $148 million in 1997 to $610 million in 1998.[1] And all this growth took place before Amazon began selling other products, such as CDs and DVDs, in 1998.

As an online bookseller, Amazon did things differently than regular bookstores. Amazon's customers couldn't flip through pages and browse as they could in a bookstore. So Amazon introduced a feature called Look Inside in 2001. It allowed users to view a book's front and back

By 1997, Amazon already had large warehouses filled with books to sell.

cover, along with the table of contents and excerpts from the text.

E-BOOKS AND TABLETS

The Amazon Kindle was not the first e-reader invented, but it has become the most popular. As early as 1997, Bezos began researching e-reader technology. At the time, people could download e-books to read on their computer, but there was no device just for books. By the early 2000s, Apple's iPod device and iTunes software were starting to dominate the digital music industry, and Bezos wanted Amazon to do the same for books.

In 2004, Bezos held a meeting and announced that he wanted Amazon to develop an e-reader. Several people in the room thought an e-reader was a terrible idea. They thought it was too costly. Plus, Amazon had no experience building hardware devices. But their protests didn't matter. Bezos threw money and resources into the project, instructing staff to create the "iPod for books." The team was called Lab126, a name based on Amazon's logo. In the logo, an arrow points from the letter *A* to the letter *Z*—from letter 1 to letter 26 in alphabetical sequence. The lab code-named the project "Fiona."

Bezos insisted on a few key features for the e-reader. He wanted a keyboard so users could easily search for books and take notes. He insisted the device be simple to use. He also wanted a digital bookstore with at least 100,000 books available for download so customers would have plenty to choose from.

Most of all, Bezos wanted the e-reader to "disappear." Bezos said books have "a feature, which I think is hard to notice but it is the books' most important feature: it disappears. When you're reading, you don't notice the

INVENTING THE KINDLE

When Lab126 started working on the Kindle, the first thing it did was look at other e-readers that had been built. E-readers weren't very popular, and Lab126 tried to figure out why. Screen quality and battery life were part of the problem. Luckily for Amazon, a new technology called E Ink had been developed. E Ink screens use millions of tiny capsules, each no wider than a strand of hair. Inside these capsules are white and black particles suspended in a clear liquid. Like a magnet, the particles have an electric charge. White has a positive charge, and black has a negative charge. The Kindle could use an electric charge to control which color floated to the top of the capsule. These little black and white particles made it easy to display crisp text on-screen. Unlike screens on most mobile devices, E Ink also works well in direct sunlight. E Ink has another advantage: excellent battery life. Electricity is only used when changing the page. This means an e-reader's battery can last for weeks or even months.

paper, the ink, the glue and the stitching. . . . All of that [disappears] and what remains is the author's world. The ability for a book to disappear became our top design objective."[2]

It took Amazon three years to finish developing the e-reader, which it called the Kindle. Amazon announced its release in November 2007 for $399. The Kindle was an immediate hit. The first batch of 25,000 sold out in just hours.[3]

Amazon not only shook up the book industry by creating the Kindle; it also changed book pricing. When Amazon introduced the Kindle, it priced the most popular e-books at $9.99, even if that meant Amazon would lose money. Amazon argued that e-books cost less to produce and readers would expect e-books to cost less. Today, e-book prices vary, but some cost as little as 99 cents, and Amazon has often battled with publishers and authors as it tries to drive book prices lower. In 2010, Amazon sold more e-books than hardcover books for the first time.

However, paper books are unlikely to vanish in the near future. E-reader sales have dropped since 2011, partly because of tablets with e-reader apps and partly because many people prefer to buy some kinds of

Bezos often introduces new models of the Kindle onstage at publicity events.

books, such as children's books, in paper format. In 2016, e-book sales dropped by almost 20 percent while sales of regular books rose.[4] Nevertheless, the Amazon Kindle has dramatically increased the spread of e-books.

In 2011, Amazon introduced its Kindle Fire tablet. The Fire, which runs on a modified version of Google's Android operating system, competes with Apple's iPad and Samsung's Galaxy Tab. True to Amazon's low-cost strategy, the Amazon Fire is much less expensive than its competitors. It is also much less capable in terms of its computing and graphics power.

SELF-PUBLISHING

When Amazon first got its start as an online bookseller, book publishers did not see it as a major competitor. It was just another bookseller that bought books to resell. In the beginning, Amazon had no warehouses full of products like it does today. Customers ordered books online from Amazon. Amazon bought the books from a large book distributor. The distributor shipped the books to Amazon, which then shipped the books to customers.

Today, Amazon not only stores and ships books in its warehouses, it also offers publishing services so authors can create their own books outside the traditional publishing industry. They can use Amazon's self-publishing services, paying Amazon to help them design, format, and print their own books. They can create print books, e-books, or even audiobooks. Then Amazon can sell the books. Instead of printing many books and then waiting for them to sell, Amazon self-publishing uses a system called print-on-demand, which means books are not produced until a customer actually orders them.

A CLEVER WORK-AROUND

In its early days, one problem Amazon ran into was that book distributors required a minimum of ten books per order. But Amazon rarely needed ten copies of a single book. Amazon found a work-around by ordering one copy of the book it needed and nine copies of an obscure book about plants called lichens. The distributors never had the unpopular lichen book in stock and just sent the one available book instead.

One author who has been very successful publishing with Amazon is science fiction writer Hugh Howey. In July 2011, Howey decided to publish his short story "Wool" as an Amazon e-book. He charged 99 cents for the story, so he didn't expect to make much money. He just kept on writing and working at a local bookstore. In October 2011, Howey noticed his book was close to selling 1,000 copies. He quickly published four more stories, all through Amazon's self-publishing service, and those sold even better. In January 2012, he published all five parts together as one novel for $5.99. By that July, Howey was selling 20,000 to 30,000 e-books a month. He was earning $150,000 a month.[5]

Howey quit his job at the bookstore and became a full-time writer. Since then he's negotiated a deal with a major New York publisher, Simon & Schuster. It will publish his books in print, and he will continue to publish his writing digitally as e-books. He also got book deals in 24 other countries, as well as a movie offer from Hollywood. Before "Wool," Howey had another book published by a small publisher. He thought about using a regular publisher for "Wool" as well. But, he explained, "I realized that all the tools were available to me. There were these new digital tools, and I could do it all myself."[6]

AMAZON MEDIA

People used to be able to watch TV and movies only if they had a TV set and a DVD player or a cable TV subscription. But high-speed internet service makes it easy for customers to stream online video to their televisions, computers, or mobile devices. Mobile video is popular, and Amazon is working hard to compete with streaming companies like Netflix and Hulu. As do many other streaming companies, Amazon now offers original movies, shows, and games. Its shows include big-budget

The Amazon Fire TV plugs into the user's television and provides access to streaming video, including content from Amazon.

dramas like *The Man in the High Castle* and acclaimed series such as *Transparent* and *Mozart in the Jungle*. Users can stream Amazon's content to their televisions using Amazon's devices, including the Amazon Fire TV and the Amazon Fire Stick.

Amazon has moved from a small online bookstore to a powerhouse media competitor. It is the biggest bookseller in the world today. The company has forever changed how people find, buy, and read books. Amazon has also changed how people shop and what they expect from an online store.

CHAPTER **FOUR**

INNOVATING THE SHOPPING EXPERIENCE

F rom the beginning, Bezos emphasized customer satisfaction—making customers happy and making things easier for them. This strategy was beneficial for customers, but it was also good for Amazon. Making shopping easier for customers increases Amazon's sales.

ONLINE INNOVATION

Today, people are used to effortless orders and fast delivery. It's easy to forget that not so long ago paying for something online with a credit card was an unfamiliar process that made people nervous. Features that seem commonplace today were brand new during Amazon's early days.

For example, Amazon let customers post online reviews. Today, reviews are virtually

Amazon helped invent the modern concept of online shopping.

everywhere online. But when Amazon first started as an online bookseller, nothing like this had ever been done before. It was a bold move. Some people worried it might be a mistake to let customers give their opinion in online reviews. What if bad reviews made sales drop?

But Bezos insisted that customer reviews would help other customers. Reviews helped shoppers make an informed choice. And because reviews helped the customer, reviews would help Amazon. Bezos wanted to give customers the power to share their opinion—good or bad—online. Today, customer reviews and comments are a standard feature on nearly all shopping websites, not just Amazon's.

EASY REORDER

Amazon.com started as an online bookseller, but Bezos always said that Amazon was not just a store. He argued Amazon was a tech company whose real business was making online shopping simpler for customers. Amazon is always looking for ways to make shopping quicker and easier. In 1997, Amazon introduced 1-Click, a way to simplify ordering. After a customer places his or her first order with a credit card and shipping address, the website automatically enables 1-Click. Then the customer can buy other things by clicking a single button. The saved credit card information and shipping address are used. Before 1-Click, customers had to reenter their payment information every time they ordered from a website. 1-Click was an online first. So Amazon applied for and received a patent for 1-Click. Having a patent meant anyone else that wanted to use this technology had to pay Amazon for it. Other companies argued that 1-Click

THE RISE OF CYBER MONDAY

As people became more comfortable with online shopping, it became part of a new retail tradition—Cyber Monday. The term *Cyber Monday* was first used in 2005 to refer to the Monday after Thanksgiving. Cyber Monday follows Black Friday, the biggest shopping day of the year. On Cyber Monday, online shopping websites—including Amazon—offer special deals on popular items.

ordering was a general business process and that the US Patent Office should never have granted a patent for it. The patent expired in 2017, allowing other companies to freely use it on their own websites.

The idea of the 1-Click ordering process led to another new Amazon idea, the Amazon Dash Button. Introduced in March 2015, Dash Buttons are an easy, one-click way to reorder products on Amazon. The Dash Button is a small wireless device a little bigger than a flash drive. Customers can get Dash Buttons for all kinds of everyday products, including laundry soap, potato chips, and toilet paper. When a person presses the button, it automatically reorders the product and charges the Amazon account. A green light on the button lets the customer know the order has been placed successfully. For example, a person could stick a Dash Button in the pantry next to his or her favorite box of crackers. When the crackers are almost gone, the user can press the Dash Button to order more instantly.

Another wireless device, the Dash Wand, uses Alexa, Amazon's voice-activated digital assistant, to help speed up orders. Users can scan a bar code or simply say the name of an item and the item is added to their Amazon

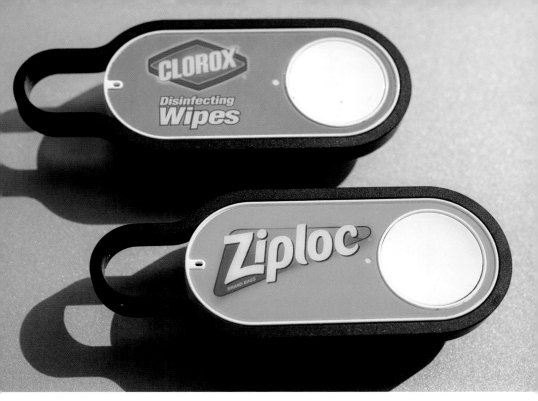

Amazon's Dash Buttons give customers a way to quickly reorder commonly used products.

shopping cart. If a person tells the Dash Wand, "Order more toothpaste," it will not only reorder it, but it will know what kind the person wants based on previous Amazon orders. The Dash Wand can also be used to search for recipes or restaurants and do other online tasks.

AMAZON PRIME

The Dash Button, Dash Wand, and other Amazon products and services are available only to customers who buy the company's premium membership, Amazon Prime. Amazon

Prime was first launched in 2005. Many of Amazon's recent innovations were developed for Amazon Prime customers. In 2018, a one-year subscription to Amazon Prime cost $119.

The membership's central feature is free two-day shipping on products sold by Amazon. It also features a variety of other perks, including music and video streaming services, photo storage, and access to Amazon's grocery delivery service. Amazon also has an annual event in July during which it runs special sales just for Prime members. In 2018, Bezos announced that more than 100 million people around the world were Amazon Prime members.[2]

In 2014, Amazon announced Prime Now, an even faster delivery service available in major cities. Prime Now offers one-hour deliveries for a fee, or two-hour free delivery.

PRIME WARDROBE AT AMAZON

There are some products customers prefer to try before purchasing. Clothes are one example. How can shoppers know if clothes will fit or look good unless they try them on? Amazon offers a service called Prime Wardrobe that is meant to solve this problem. With Prime Wardrobe, customers can pick three or more items from Amazon to be shipped to them. They have seven days to try everything on. They decide what they want to keep, pay for those items online, then send what they don't want back to Amazon in a resealable, prepaid box.

The Amazon Prime Now service relies on a delivery network that can deliver orders to customers within an hour or two.

By 2018, Prime Now was available in 32 US metropolitan areas.[3]

SELLING WITH AMAZON

Two other programs also help drive customers to Amazon: Amazon Marketplace and Amazon Associates. With Amazon Marketplace, launched in 2000, individuals or businesses can sell their merchandise on Amazon's site, right alongside Amazon's products. Marketplace sellers pay Amazon a small percentage of the sale. With Amazon Associates, individuals or businesses can place links to Amazon product pages on their websites. If a user clicks the link and buys the item on Amazon, the Associate gets a small percentage of the sale. This program started in 1996, when a customer wrote and asked for permission to link book reviews from her website to Amazon's site so that people could buy the books. These earnings can add up over time. In 2009, blogger Darren Rowse posted that his photography blog had earned $119,725.45 since he joined the Associates program in 2003.[4] He also offered tips about how other bloggers could earn money by joining the Associates program.

The more products and services Amazon offers, the more customers it can get and keep. And the more customers it has, the more it can analyze customer preferences and study how to win even more customers. Amazon can easily track how much time people spent on the website, what people buy, and how much they spend. Amazon then analyzes this information to find new ways to get and keep customers on its site.

SEARS AND RETAIL HISTORY

In many ways, Amazon's use of technology to create an innovative shopping experience is not new. The same thing was done more than a century ago by Sears, Roebuck, and Company. In the 1890s, the company took advantage of improving mail service, transportation infrastructure, and communications technology. It produced a 500-page order-by-mail catalog. No longer did customers have to come to a store. They could order through the mail and have products shipped directly to them. Like Amazon, the Sears catalog said that customer satisfaction was its number one priority, and like Amazon, Sears tightly controlled costs. Sears also started out without any physical stores, but eventually it started opening stores where it could sell its goods.

In 2018, Sears closed many of its stores, thanks in part to the emergence of online retailers like Amazon. However, the companies forged a new partnership in that year as well. Sears announced in June that customers would be able to purchase car tires on Amazon and then have them installed at Sears's service centers.

CHAPTER **FIVE**

REINVENTING DELIVERY

O ne of Amazon's major focuses in improving the customer experience has been in speeding up delivery. Free two-day shipping is one of the main reasons Amazon Prime is so popular. Amazon has changed expectations for delivery time in modern online shopping.

Originally, Amazon wasn't always so speedy. It had no warehouses because it had no inventory. It bought books and then resold them directly to customers. But Amazon couldn't always count on book publishers and distributors to get books to them on time. In its early days, Amazon's book delivery could take anywhere from one day to two weeks, depending on availability. Early employees packed books into shipping boxes until two or three o'clock in the morning.

Amazon demonstrated its latest package-delivery initiative to journalists in Seattle in 2018.

And orders were growing rapidly. Bezos knew quick delivery was important to his customers.

FULFILLMENT CENTERS

In 1997, Amazon began storing books in its own warehouse, called a fulfillment center. Later that year, Bezos announced that Amazon would dramatically increase the size of its Seattle warehouse and build a new warehouse in Delaware. Bezos wanted fulfillment centers that were far more than just giant storage units. He wanted his fulfillment centers to quickly sort books, pull together orders, package them, and mail them.

At the time, Walmart had the best distribution network in the world. So in 1998, Bezos hired Jimmy Wright, a retired Walmart vice president, to fix Amazon's fulfillment problems. A distribution network consists of all the interconnected steps involved to get a product from a factory to the shelf of a store. As one of the biggest retailers in the United States, Walmart had a huge network of distribution centers—warehouses where products were stored and then transferred for shipment to stores.

Bezos told Wright they needed ten times the space they currently had and they needed to be able to ship just about anything. Amazon was getting ready to sell much more than books, and Amazon sales were growing three times bigger every year.

The 1998 holiday season was hectic. Every employee from the main office worked at least one nighttime shift filling and packaging orders. The emergency packing operation was called "Save Santa."[1] People arrived at midnight, bringing family and friends to help. Some slept in their cars for a few hours before going back to their regular jobs. When the temporary help walked into the warehouse, they were met at the door by an orange-vested manager in work boots. There were giant packing stations on one side and miles and vast rows of shelves on the other. The books were not shelved in any kind of order. However, each location on the shelves had a bar code, so a computer could track down every book.

BEZOS'S VALUES

Bezos is a big fan of Sam Walton, the founder of Walmart. In his biography, *Sam Walton: Made in America*, Walton expressed many of the values Bezos believes in: frugality, action, borrowing good ideas from competitors, and constantly questioning his company's current business methods. To encourage Amazon's employees to be active in improving the company, Bezos gives out an award to an employee who does something valuable for Amazon without being asked. The trophy for the award is an old pair of size 15 Nike sneakers that had belonged to Dan Kraft, an Amazon engineer who had once played basketball for Northwestern University.

Amazon's fulfillment centers are packed with goods, along with the workers and machinery needed to move them from place to place.

Workers called pickers grabbed a computer-generated list of books and a wheeled cart. The list guided the picker through the shelves from one book to another along the quickest possible route. Pickers piled the books on their cart, weaving in and out of the traffic from other carts. When the list was complete, pickers turned in the list and received a score based on how many books they picked per minute. Then they grabbed another list and headed out again, trying to beat their high score. All night long, they picked and packed books.

Wright spent $300 million dollars building and updating fulfillment centers with conveyor belts, blinking lights that guided pickers, and scanning and sorting machines.[2] But even with seven fulfillment centers, the 1999 holiday season brought the same problems and another Operation Save Santa. In the end, Amazon decided it would have to create its own system for its unique needs. Its engineers and researchers developed a fast, efficient, and accurate system to help make its operations run more smoothly.

Amazon's fulfillment centers are massive. In 2016, Amazon hired 120,000 temporary workers to meet the holiday shopping rush.[3] One fulfillment center in Washington shipped one million packages in 24 hours.[4]

INSIDE FULFILLMENT CENTERS

Amazon has more than 75 fulfillment centers in North America. These warehouses are huge. One of Amazon's four fulfillment centers in Phoenix, Arizona, has been described by the *Economist* as the "Grand Canyon with a roof."[5] It can easily fit 20 football fields inside it. Amazon's fulfillment centers are busiest over the holidays. During the peak season of November and December, employees sometimes work 12-hour days. Employees called pickers receive orders on a handheld scanner called a pick mod. The pick mod guides the pickers to each item. Items are scanned, put into tote bags, and then sent by conveyor belt to workers called packers. Packers use computer-generated formulas to determine the correct type of box for each order. Amazon also uses robots to help move merchandise and speed up the process.

FULFILLMENT BY AMAZON

In 2006, Amazon introduced a new service called Fulfillment by Amazon. Amazon advertises this service as, "You sell it, we ship it." Any individual or business can store its products in Amazon's warehouses, and Amazon will "pick, pack and ship" the order.[6] Just as Amazon did when it let other sellers pay to place their books and products on Amazon, Amazon also lets other sellers pay to use its warehouse space. Amazon is an expert at packing and shipping packages at a low cost, and others can pay for this expertise.

One company that uses Fulfillment by Amazon is Tech Armor. Tech Armor makes protective phone and tablet cases. On its first day of business, Tech Armor sold only two phone cases. But the company grew quickly.

PRIME AIR

Amazon ships so many packages that it leases its own fleet of airplanes. In 2016, Amazon revealed its first Prime Air plane, a Boeing 767. Its Prime Air cargo aircraft are painted with "Prime Air" on the side and an Amazon logo on the plane's belly that can be seen when the planes are in the air.

Amazon's goal is to have these additional aircraft available to deliver packages during peak periods. These planes can also help meet additional shipping needs for Amazon's popular Prime membership, with its free two-day shipping. Leasing its own airplanes means Amazon can better control where and when the planes fly and what they carry. For example, planes can transport goods from one fulfillment center to another. Amazon also leases semitrucks and cargo ships.

Six months later, Tech Armor had $3 million worth of business. It decided to use Fulfillment by Amazon so it could grow quickly and offer customers the fast, free shipping they wanted.

NEW DELIVERY OPTIONS

Amazon is known for its quick delivery, but some customers do not want packages left on their doorstep due to the risk of theft. Amazon offers two services designed to keep packages safe. The first one is called Amazon Locker. Started in 2011, Amazon Locker is a structure containing multiple individual lockers. Packages are delivered to the lockers, and customers can access the locker containing their package by entering a special code. Amazon Lockers are usually located inside malls or grocery stores.

In 2017, Amazon also started a service called Hub, which is similar to Amazon Lockers but for residential buildings like apartments. A Hub unit is a large cabinet with 42 lockers. Building owners pay Amazon to have a Hub installed in the building. It can be used for any package delivery, not just delivery from Amazon.

order
online
pick up
here

bazaar

Amazon Lockers were present in more than 50 cities by 2018.

In addition to lockers, Amazon has developed a new device that customers can install in their homes to help with package delivery. It's called Amazon Key. Available to Amazon Prime members in some cities, Amazon Key includes a smart lock, a security camera, and an app. The camera can communicate with the lock. When an Amazon delivery shows up at a house, the driver scans a bar code on the package. This sends a notification to the app, telling it to turn on the camera. Once the camera is on, the driver sends a signal that unlocks the smart lock and lets the driver into the house to deliver the package. The driver sends another signal to lock the smart lock when leaving. Amazon notifies customers that the delivery has been made and sends them the video.

There have been concerns about Amazon Key. Some security companies have shown that the lock and the camera can be hacked. There are also privacy concerns. With Amazon Key, the customer gives Amazon control over a camera in the house. Amazon says it will never use the camera to spy on customers, but security breaches and poor corporate behavior have left many consumers skeptical of large technology companies. Some people argue that it's too risky to give Amazon access to your home and privacy.

AMAZON FLEX

Started in 2015, Amazon Flex is a delivery program that lets people sign up to deliver packages for Amazon. It's kind of like being an Uber or Lyft driver for Amazon. Amazon established the program to help with "last mile" deliveries. This part of delivery—the final leg, in which packages are dropped off at customers' homes—is the most difficult part of the delivery process because packages must travel to so many different final destinations. By early 2018, the program existed in 50 cities. It is a way for Amazon to manage fluctuating delivery needs. Amazon Flex drivers use their own cars and pay for their own gas. They download the Amazon Flex app to their own smartphones, and they use the app to scan packages, map their route, and confirm order delivery. Drivers check the app to see if delivery work is available. Pay, pickup locations, and amount of delivery time required can vary depending on the assignment.

CHAPTER SIX

RETAIL EXPERIMENTS

A s physical bookstores, including the Borders chain, have closed over the past several years, many booksellers have blamed Amazon. The company had achieved great success in online retailing, so when it announced in 2015 that it was opening Amazon Books, a physical store in Seattle, many were surprised. Amazon's physical bookstore is a lot like any other bookstore, but it has a few key differences. First, none of the books have price tags. The book prices are constantly changing, depending on how much they cost on the Amazon website. Customers cannot spend cash at the store—they must use a credit card or the Amazon smartphone app.

On the bookshelves, all the books are arranged with the cover facing out. None are shelved like library books, with the spine out.

The introduction of Amazon Books stores demonstrated that Amazon felt it could bring a new experience to retail shopping.

There's a bookshelf for books personally recommended by Bezos, which includes a novel written by his wife, MacKenzie. The "bestseller" bookshelf features the current top sellers on Amazon. The store also sells all of Amazon's devices, including Kindle e-readers and Fire tablets.

By early 2018, Amazon had 15 Amazon Books locations and plans for three more.[1] Business experts wondered why Amazon would bother opening physical bookstores. Some believed the company wanted to learn more about customers' buying habits. Others thought Amazon needed a place for people to try out its tech gadgets.

In 2017, Amazon bought the supermarket company Whole Foods Market. Many business experts continued to wonder why Amazon, an online giant, wanted to own physical stores. But it soon became clear that Amazon's physical presence would also benefit what the company does online. Amazon doesn't use Whole Foods to simply

THE DECLINE OF PAPER BOOKS?

In the late 1990s, Bezos predicted, "I firmly believe that at some point the vast majority of books will be in electronic form. I also believe that is a long way in the future, many more than ten years in the future."[2] So far his prediction has not come true. In 2015, e-book sales beat regular books. But in 2016, e-book sales dropped sharply, and paper books were on top once again.

sell organic groceries. Now when customers go to Whole Foods, they can buy Amazon devices or an Amazon Prime membership. Amazon has also installed Amazon Lockers. Customers with Amazon Prime memberships get special discounts on groceries. Amazon incorporated Whole Foods into its existing grocery delivery service, Amazon Fresh. Amazon also started dropping prices sharply to beat out other grocery chains.

AMAZON GO

Though a tech giant owns them, Amazon Books and Whole Foods feel mostly like any other retail stores. But another experimental project, the Amazon Go store, is like nothing that has existed in retailing before. Amazon Go is a small grocery store located next to Amazon's main headquarters in Seattle. It opened to the public in 2018. There are no cashiers or checkout lines. Customers walk in, grab the items they want, and leave. Their credit cards are charged automatically for the items they took.

THE POWER OF PHYSICAL STORES

Despite the power of online shopping, most shopping still happens in physical stores. One study found that 90 percent of all retail sales occur in stores, and only 5 percent of retail sales are completely online.[3] Every year online shopping grows, but people still prefer to shop in stores, where they can see and hold physical goods before buying them.

The Amazon Go store is a high-tech wonder that uses an array of sensors and cameras, computer vision, and machine learning. To shop at Amazon Go, a customer needs an Amazon account and Amazon's smartphone app. When walking into the store, the customer swipes his or her phone over an electronic scanner. Cameras and sensors in the ceiling and on the shelves monitor what the customer does. If they see a person pick up an item, Amazon adds it to a virtual shopping cart. If the person puts the item back, Amazon removes it from the cart. When the customer leaves, Amazon charges him or her for all the items that were taken and sends a receipt. The receipt even shows exactly how much time was spent shopping, perhaps to help remind people how quick it is to shop at Amazon Go.

It's a strange feeling to just walk out of a store without stopping to pay at the cash register. In fact, the first time customers shop at Amazon Go, they often say it feels like shoplifting because they simply take things off the shelves and walk out. Amazon even has signs near the exit to reassure people, saying, "Just walk out shopping" and "Thanks for shopping. You're good to go (really)."[4]

A vast array of cameras and sensors looks down upon Amazon Go customers to track what they are picking up and purchasing.

Amazon knows who customers are from the moment they enter the store, and it then tracks everything the customers do. Amazon can use all this data to learn even more about people's unique buying habits and patterns. It learns what kinds of products people pull off the shelf and which ones they put back. It tracks how long people spend in certain parts of the store. Eventually, Amazon may be able to offer virtual coupons based on customers' shopping patterns while they are in the store. The company believes that Amazon Go represents the future of the retail experience.

CHAPTER SEVEN

AMAZON AND TECHNOLOGY

When Bezos was a kid, he loved reading science fiction novels and watching *Star Trek*. He taught himself how to write computer code and spent hours playing a *Star Trek* game on a school computer. Once upon a time, artificial intelligence, drones, and robots sounded like things out of a science fiction novel. Not anymore. Bezos has built his online bookstore into a huge company that is a world leader in technology research and development. Amazon's goal is to use this technology to speed up and improve how it delivers its products and services.

PRIME AIR

One way to make deliveries faster is to avoid roads and traffic altogether. As drone technology became increasingly popular in the 2010s,

Amazon showed off a prototype of its drone delivery system in 2015.

Amazon studied how these flying devices might be able to carry goods directly to customers' homes. The project became known as Prime Air.

Bezos first announced the idea of Prime Air drone delivery in 2013. On the television news show *60 Minutes*, Bezos gave viewers a sneak peek at Amazon's experimental drones and how they might work. However, the technology did not roll out right away. By 2018, drone deliveries were not yet taking place on a large scale. One of Amazon's biggest challenges has been working through the complex regulations needed to ensure people's safety. In the United States, the Federal Aviation Administration (FAA) is the government agency that controls air traffic and safety laws. The FAA is very interested in drones, in part because drone traffic can pose a risk to airplanes. The FAA decides what drones are allowed to do in US airspace. In 2014, Amazon asked the FAA for permission to start testing Prime Air drones outside. But the FAA did not respond right away, so Amazon began its testing in the United Kingdom, where regulations were not as strict.

On December 7, 2016, Amazon carried out its first official drone delivery. A customer in Cambridge, England, was specially chosen. Amazon picked a customer with a

large yard who lived near an
Amazon distribution center.
The customer placed an order
for an Amazon Fire Stick
and some popcorn. Thirteen
minutes later, a drone dropped
off the package in the yard.

Amazon's drones are
designed to fly up to 400 feet
(122 m) above the ground.
This is well above people
and most buildings, but still
100 feet (30 m) lower than the
minimum for small airplanes.
Battery operated, the drones
can fly at more than 60 miles
per hour (97 kmh) and make a round trip as far as 20 miles
(32 km).[1] According to Amazon, approximately 85 percent
of the products on its website are light enough, about
five pounds (2.2 kg) or less, to be delivered by drone.[2]
In addition to developing the drones itself, Amazon will
also need to create a computer control system to manage
drone traffic. This will be especially important if drone
delivery becomes a widespread service.

FAA DRONE REGULATIONS

Under FAA regulations, unmanned drones must weigh less than 55 pounds (25 kg).[3] The drone must remain in sight of the operator, and the drone operator can use only one drone at a time. Drone operators can fly only during the day, and they are not allowed to fly in areas with heavy air traffic or in airspace that is restricted for security reasons, such as certain parts of Washington, DC. Because these FAA regulations are stricter than those in some other countries, US companies that want to test drones often do so outside of the United States.

AMAZON ROBOTICS

At an Amazon fulfillment center in Washington State, trucks unload packages onto a giant conveyor belt called a vision tunnel. This tunnel features scanners that take pictures of packages and upload this information to Amazon's computers. These machines can process thousands of products coming into the warehouse twice as fast as a human can with a handheld scanner.[4]

In the center of this fulfillment center is a yellow robot. Strong enough to lift a car, this giant robot does work that is too difficult for humans. It picks up heavy pallets loaded with boxes and lifts them to the second floor of the warehouse, where they will stay until it is time to ship them.

At this enormous warehouse, driverless vehicles instead of forklifts with drivers sometimes tow boxes. Other robots called Kivas, wheeled machines that look a little like oversized robot vacuum cleaners, move shelves closer to the employees. The Kivas make it faster for workers to pick and pack items.

As part of Amazon's efforts to make fulfillment centers more efficient, Amazon bought the company Kiva Systems in 2012 for $775 million.[5] It has taken years for Amazon

Powerful robotic arms do the heavy lifting inside Amazon
fulfillment centers.

to figure out the best way to integrate these robots into fulfillment centers. Some people fear that all these robots will replace human jobs. Amazon says these new, more automated fulfillment centers need more humans because these warehouses can store so much more. Others say that robots are doing the warehouse work that people don't want to do anyway.

In the past few years, Amazon has sponsored the Amazon Robotics Challenge. Started in 2015 as a way to "promote shared and open solutions" to automating typical warehouse tasks, the contest has a $250,000 prize.[6] This competition is part of RoboCup, an international robotics competition. Surprisingly, one of the very hardest tasks for robots is grasping and picking up items. Boxes are relatively easy. Odd-shaped items are much harder. It's also a challenge for robots to pick up items one after another if they have different shapes. It may be easy for a human to pick up a pencil, a paper plate, and a ball one after another, but that's a big challenge for a robot. Experts believed it would be several years before robots able to pick up such varied objects were available commercially.

ECHO AND ALEXA

Today, several tech companies have their own digital assistants. Apple's devices have Siri. Microsoft's have Cortana. Google's is simply named Google Assistant. Amazon's assistant, featured in its Echo speaker device, is named Alexa. Amazon released its Echo speaker in the fall of 2014. Coming on the heels of the summer 2014 failure of the Fire Phone, the Echo developers felt tremendous pressure to succeed. Lab126, the same lab that developed the Kindle and Fire Phone, created the Echo speaker.

Robots move racks of merchandise throughout Amazon fulfillment centers.

There is no touch screen or keyboard for the Echo. The only way to activate it is to speak to its "virtual assistant," Alexa. Amazon's goal is for Alexa to communicate as easily and naturally as humans do. This goal can be challenging. It can be difficult for a computer to tell the difference between background noise and true communication. Another challenge is learning all the different possible actions a person may want. A user may want to play movies, shop, ask for general information, or call a friend. A huge variety of combinations of words and phrases may be used for these tasks.

Artificial intelligence systems like Alexa use speech recognition and machine learning to approach this challenging job. Speech recognition breaks down the sounds of a person's voice and then matches them with the corresponding words. Machine learning is when a

FIRE PHONE FLAMEOUT

One of Amazon's biggest failed experiments was a smartphone. In 2014, Amazon introduced a phone called the Fire Phone. Unlike Amazon's usual low-cost products, the Fire Phone was costly at $650. Amazon had signed an exclusive deal with the phone company AT&T, so users could only get the phone if they had AT&T as their cell phone service provider. Within two months, AT&T was offering the phone for just 99 cents with a two-year contract. One month later, Amazon reported that it had lost $170 million on the Fire Phone and had $83 million worth of Fire Phones sitting in warehouses that nobody wanted to buy.[7]

Amazon executive David Limp introduced new Echo models at an event in 2017.

computer system has the ability to learn and improve from experience, without being programmed with exactly what to do.

A few basic rules help guide Alexa's behavior. First, it has "wake words" that trigger it to start actively listening to the user. Alexa converts this speech into text. After deciding when the user has stopped talking, Alexa interprets the request and decides what to do. If it can't figure out what to do, it asks more questions.

AMAZON WEB SERVICES

Amazon Web Services (AWS) is Amazon's cloud computing platform. Cloud computing is the ability to use remote computing services that users access over the internet. Rather than store or process data on a machine that the user owns, it can be cheaper to simply rent the storage and computing time from someone else.

AWS works a bit like an electricity company. An electricity company provides customers with access to a huge electric grid, but it charges customers only for the energy they use. AWS works the same way. Customers pay only for the computing power they use. During peak times, like when a website is streaming video of a major event, a company pays for the extra computing power it needs to handle the extra website traffic. When website traffic is lighter, it pays less. With AWS, companies don't have to worry about buying and maintaining so many computers themselves.

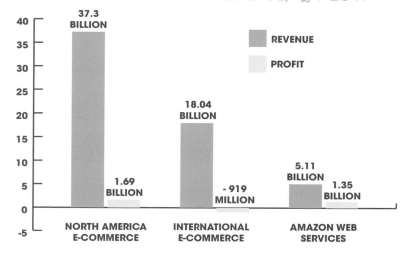

AWS AND AMAZON'S REVENUE, Q4 2017[10]

37.3 BILLION — NORTH AMERICA E-COMMERCE (REVENUE)
1.69 BILLION — NORTH AMERICA E-COMMERCE (PROFIT)
18.04 BILLION — INTERNATIONAL E-COMMERCE (REVENUE)
- 919 MILLION — INTERNATIONAL E-COMMERCE (PROFIT)
5.11 BILLION — AMAZON WEB SERVICES (REVENUE)
1.35 BILLION — AMAZON WEB SERVICES (PROFIT)

REVENUE
PROFIT

In the fourth quarter of 2017, Amazon lost money in its international e-commerce business, but profits from Amazon Web Services more than made up for that deficit. AWS has proven to be an extremely successful and profitable business for the company.

Like other services Amazon offers, AWS started as a service that Amazon needed for its own business. Eventually Amazon decided to let other companies buy this same service. AWS began in 2006, and today it powers businesses in 190 countries.[8] Netflix, Pinterest, the National Aeronautics and Space Administration (NASA), the Central Intelligence Agency (CIA), and many other organizations use AWS. By 2017, AWS provided more than 40 percent of all cloud computing services available online.[9]

CHAPTER **EIGHT**

CRITICISMS OF AMAZON

From its earliest days as a start-up company, Amazon has always demanded a lot from its employees. It is known as a frugal workplace with long hours and few perks. Some employees like the challenge of Amazon's fast-paced, hard-driving environment. But there have also been reports that Amazon has gone too far in pushing its employees.

TROUBLE AT FULFILLMENT CENTERS

On July 25, 2011, a security guard reported unsafe conditions at the eastern Pennsylvania Amazon fulfillment center where he worked. He said temperatures in the warehouse were over 110 degrees Fahrenheit (43°C). He reported that two pregnant women, both warehouse workers, had gone to see nurses because of the heat,

Working conditions inside Amazon's fulfillment centers have attracted controversy.

and that Amazon refused to open doors that might help cool the warehouse down. The security guard reported these concerns to the Occupational Safety and Health Administration (OSHA), a US government agency in charge of investigating unsafe workplace conditions.

The security guard's report was not the first complaint filed against Amazon that summer. It had been a brutally hot summer, and the warehouse had no air-conditioning. Throughout June 2011, OSHA received other complaints about excessive heat in the fulfillment center, including one from an emergency room doctor. The doctor reported that his hospital had treated several patients for heat-related injuries they had received while at work in Amazon's fulfillment center. One worker reported blurred vision. Another reported dizziness and leg cramps. A worker said he saw one coworker pass out at the water fountain and other coworkers helped out of the overheated warehouse by paramedics using wheelchairs and stretchers.

An Amazon manager said during extreme heat the company gave workers five-minute breaks every hour. Employees said this was not the case. They got only two 15-minute breaks during their ten-hour work shifts.

OSHA came to investigate the complaints. Amazon eventually added more fans. The following year it said it would install air-conditioning in more fulfillment centers.

Workers at this fulfillment center said they were afraid they would be fired if they stopped to rest during the heat. One worker said he had done well for the first six months, and then one day Amazon doubled the number of units he had to pick from 250 per hour to 500 per hour.[1] He said that since he was relatively young, he could keep up, but many of the older workers couldn't. Those workers got negative reviews on their work records. Too many negative reviews lead to workers losing their jobs. One worker in his fifties said he was expected to pick 1,200 items during his work shift, which works out to one item every 30 seconds. He said he had to get on his hands and knees 250 to 300 times a day just to reach items in

DEATHS AT FULFILLMENT CENTERS

In September 2017, two Amazon workers were killed at two different fulfillment centers, one in Pennsylvania and one in Indiana. According to EHS (Environmental Health and Safety), an organization focused on employee safety, since 2013 a total of five Amazon workers have been killed while working in fulfillment centers: "Two workers have been crushed to death by forklifts, one dragged into a conveyor belt, another crushed by a pallet loader and one run over by a truck."[2] In North America, Amazon has more than 75 fulfillment centers with more than 125,000 full-time Amazon employees.[3]

their bins.[4] He won gift cards and a laptop for being a good employee, but he was also written up for not being fast enough. Eventually he was fired.

These are examples from one fulfillment center in Pennsylvania. Amazon declined to discuss the situation with the newspaper that reported it, the *Morning Call* of Allentown, Pennsylvania. But these examples are not unique. There have been many news reports about the difficult working conditions at fulfillment centers around the world.

TROUBLE AT THE OFFICE

Jobs in Amazon's warehouses are physically demanding. But employees in Amazon's offices have also reported problems. On August 15, 2015, the *New York Times* published an article titled "Inside Amazon: Wrestling Big Ideas in a Bruising Workplace." Two reporters interviewed more than 100 former and current Amazon employees about what it was like to work at Amazon.

Amazon is known as a highly competitive place to work where employees are pushed to their limits. One former employee described Amazon as "the greatest place I hate to work."[7]

Many of the employees interviewed felt Amazon went too far in its demands from employees. One employee said, "Nearly every person I worked with, I saw cry at their desk."[8] Another employee commented, "I didn't see a whole lot of crying at desks. But I did see a lot of crying in bathrooms."[9]

Another employee, who worked selling Amazon gift cards to other companies, went as long as four straight days with no sleep. Eventually, the stress gave her an ulcer. Amazon didn't force her to work this hard. But this was the price required to succeed at her job.

One woman received high work ratings for years. Then her father got cancer, and she started traveling to care for him. She could no longer work the 80-hour weeks her job demanded. She said she couldn't transfer to a lighter job, and she said her boss called her a "problem." She eventually took unpaid leave to care for her father. She never returned to Amazon.

Amazon's corporate offices have gained a reputation among some as stressful, high-pressure workplaces.

The *New York Times* gave dozens of examples about the harsh conditions at Amazon. Bezos responded to the article in a letter he wrote to his employees. He said, "I don't recognize this Amazon and I very much hope you don't, either."[10] He said if any employees knew about this kind of treatment, they should contact him directly. In response to the *Times* article, some employees posted online about their positive experiences working for Amazon. Some said that Amazon had been harsh in the past but had improved.

The bad publicity from these events has led to changes at Amazon. The high demand for tech workers has also forced Amazon to improve its office work environment to stay competitive and attract talent. Nevertheless, many employees say that the heavy workload and stressful work is intentional, and the result is that only the most committed employees survive.

CRUSHING COMPETITION

Amazon started out small, but today it is a huge company. Now that Amazon is one of the biggest companies in the world, some say it has an unfair advantage. A large percentage of traffic on the internet runs on AWS. Even Amazon's competitors use AWS. Amazon sells millions of products online. Many stores that compete with Amazon also pay Amazon for services like AWS, Fulfillment by Amazon, or the Amazon Associates program.

Online shopping accounts for only approximately 10 percent of retail sales, but more than 50 percent of all Americans shop on Amazon.[11] When Amazon says it is moving into a new area, stock prices for other competing brands usually drop. For example, when Amazon bought Whole Foods, grocery-chain stocks dropped immediately. Some business experts and government officials fear that Amazon's size and influence might smother other companies and prevent healthy business competition.

AMAZON AND THE PUBLISHING INDUSTRY

Amazon has long come under harsh criticism by the publishing industry for its practices in bookselling. In 2017, a new development brought this matter into the foreground again. Amazon changed the "buy" option on the product pages for its books so that it didn't always lead to the new copies of the book distributed by Amazon on behalf of the publisher. Instead, an algorithm on the website decided whether Amazon or a selected third-party seller would get the sale. Third-party sellers often offer books at a discount, but the publishing industry railed against this change. The Authors Guild, an industry group, explained, "The problem with this outcome from an author's perspective is that neither the publisher nor the author gets a cent back from those third-party sales. Only Amazon and the reseller share in the profits."[12]

The industry continued to track this change in 2018. *Publishers Weekly* wrote about a follow-up study that found that third-party sellers won the buy button approximately 5 percent of the time.[13] Some of the third-party sellers were offering early review copies of books that publishers had sent out. In response, some

Amazon's pricing and sales practices for both e-books and print books have come under fire by the publishing industry.

publishers added notes on these books prohibiting them from resale.

PAYING ITS FAIR SHARE?

Many big companies find ways to pay as little tax as possible, and Amazon is no exception. Amazon has always made every effort to avoid paying taxes by taking advantage of laws that don't apply to online sales. When Bezos started Amazon, he considered locating Amazon in California. But he decided on Seattle, in part so that he could avoid charging state sales tax. Sales tax is the tax you pay when you buy an item at a store. Because out-of-state customers don't have to pay state sales tax, and Washington had a relatively small population, fewer customers would have to pay sales tax on the books they ordered. No sales tax meant lower prices for customers, giving Amazon an advantage over physical stores that did have to charge sales tax.

As online shopping grew, states started requiring sales tax for online companies, but Amazon has fought to avoid collecting it. As of 2017, Amazon has started collecting sales tax for all states that have sales tax (not all states do), but Amazon does not collect sales tax for the sellers who use Amazon Fulfillment to sell their own products. These sellers are supposed to collect the sales tax themselves, but many of these small sellers don't. Amazon earns money from the fees it charges these sellers without having to worry about collecting sales tax.

Changes to online sales tax laws appeared to be on the horizon in 2018. In July, the Supreme Court ruled that retailers can be required to collect sales tax from customers, even if the company has no physical presence

Sales tax policy changes were expected to affect many online retailers, including independent businesses that sell their products through Amazon.

in the customer's state. Brick-and-mortar retailers praised the decision, which they felt would level the playing field.

Amazon pays almost no federal tax, despite being worth over $700 billion.[14] Amazon avoids US federal taxes by using legal tax credits and exemptions. For example, it can use R&D (research and development) tax credits to subtract some of the cost of developing new technology.

Amazon also avoids paying taxes by negotiating special tax breaks from states and local communities. For example, when Amazon began searching for a location for its second headquarters in 2017, many cities and states offered the company steep tax breaks in the hope that Amazon would choose them. For instance, New Jersey offered $7 billion in tax breaks if Amazon picked a location near Newark, New Jersey. States have given Amazon more than $600 million in state tax breaks for building its existing fulfillment centers, and another $147 million for data centers.[15]

In 2017, Amazon paid no US federal income taxes at all, even though the company made $5.6 billion in US profits.[16] Amazon is not doing anything illegal, and many companies use similar strategies to legally avoid taxes. However, given Amazon's extraordinary profits, some people feel that Amazon is not "playing fair" and should

BIDDING FOR HQ2

In 2017, Amazon announced plans to build a second headquarters outside of Seattle. The new headquarters has been nicknamed HQ2. Amazon said it would invest $5 billion in HQ2 and that it would provide 50,000 new jobs over ten years. Amazon let cities apply for the chance to be picked as the new location. Amazon received more than 200 proposals. These applications often included tax breaks for Amazon. Newark offered a tax break as high as $7 billion. Chicago offered to let Amazon keep over $1 billion in income taxes.[17]

have to pay more in taxes. Economist Matthew Gardner says, "More so than any company I can think of, Amazon appears to have built their profit maximization strategy around avoiding taxes at various levels."[18]

CONFLICT WITH THE PRESIDENT

On December 29, 2017, President Donald Trump tweeted a sharp criticism of Amazon: "Why is the United States Post Office, which is losing many billions of dollars a year, while charging Amazon and others so little to deliver their packages, making Amazon richer and the Post Office dumber and poorer? Should be charging MUCH MORE!"[19] This was just one in a series of statements he made charging that Amazon was taking advantage of the US Postal Service by getting unfairly low rates for delivery.

Industry analysts disputed this contention, noting that by law, the Postal Service is required to ensure that its shipping deals with companies are profitable. In an article about Trump's criticism of Amazon, the *Verge* noted, "Trump's feud with Amazon is often seen as a proxy war on Bezos and the *Post*," referring to the *Washington Post*, which Bezos bought in 2013.[20] The *Washington Post* has published articles and opinion pieces critical of Trump and his administration.

President Trump met in person with Bezos and other American technology company leaders, including Microsoft CEO Satya Nadella, *center*, in June 2017.

ALEXA AND PRIVACY

Amazon's Echo, along with other smart devices, has come under intense scrutiny for its privacy implications. Many users worry about having an always-listening microphone present in their home. Amazon has insisted that users are safe using the device, but a few incidents have cast doubt over the idea that a personal voice assistant can be truly private and secure.

In 2017, security researchers found that a person with physical access to another person's Echo could set it up to secretly record conversations. In 2018, an Oregon woman was surprised when audio clips of a conversation she had with her husband were recorded and sent to a person on her contacts list. Amazon explained that this recording and sending feature must have been triggered accidentally by voice commands that were mistaken or misunderstood. In a statement, it said, "As unlikely as this string of events is, we are evaluating options to make this case even less likely."[21]

BLOCKING PHONES

In 2017, Amazon received a patent for a device that could block in-store customers from using their smartphones to compare prices online. The patent is called "Physical Store Online Shopping Control." The device can block search terms and website requests when a customer is using in-store wireless internet service. So if, for example, a person is in Amazon Go buying milk and wants to see if Walmart sells milk for less, Amazon's device could block the person's access to Walmart's website. Alternatively, it could compare prices and then send an in-store coupon. The device even has a way to locate a person in the store in case Amazon wanted to suggest another item or direct a sales clerk over to help the customer.

CHAPTER NINE

THE FUTURE OF AMAZON

As of 2018, Amazon has made Bezos the richest man in the world. The small online bookstore he founded in 1994 has grown to become one of the most powerful companies on the planet. Bezos's insistence on innovation and experimentation have been key ingredients in Amazon's success.

TWITCH

Amazon has branched out far beyond its original mission of selling books. The company creates devices, provides online services, and even produces original television series. Still, a decision the company made in August 2014 confused some industry analysts. In that month, Amazon paid $970 million to purchase Twitch, a website that streams live video of users

Twitch represented one of Amazon's largest purchases ever.

playing video games.[1] It seemed like a big investment for something outside of Amazon's main business.

However, over the next few years it became clear that Twitch was an important part of Amazon's future as a technology company. Streaming video from Twitch's more than 100 million users requires a strong internet infrastructure—the same kind of infrastructure that powers AWS. As Amazon competes with other tech giants, including Facebook, Google, and Microsoft, industry journalist Matt Weinberger notes, "Twitch could be a huge competitive advantage for Amazon Web Services."[2] Amazon's continued investment in Twitch suggests that technology remains a core component of the company's future.

HEALTH CARE

Amazon's work with machine learning and artificial intelligence, seen in its

TWITCH AND GAME STREAMING

Streaming games online has rapidly become a huge industry in the United States and around the world. Twitch has been a big part of that growth, and by 2017 it was by far the largest streaming platform, making up 37 percent of total game-streaming revenue.[3] After Amazon purchased Twitch, it made some changes to help integrate the service into other Amazon offerings. While watching a streamer, users can now click a button on the page to purchase the game being played from Amazon. Amazon Prime subscribers also get benefits on Twitch, earning exclusive in-game items.

Echo devices and its Alexa digital assistant, has led the company in new directions. In October 2016, Bezos suggested where Amazon might be headed in the future: "I think healthcare is going to be one of those industries that is elevated and made better by machine learning and artificial intelligence. And I actually think Echo and Alexa do have a role to play in that."[4]

The next summer, in July 2017, Amazon set up a new group within the company to study health-care technology, calling it Lab1492. The company released no details on what the group would be working on, though experts speculated it might develop new apps or devices that apply artificial intelligence to help both patients and doctors.

The company's interest in health care goes beyond this secretive lab. In February 2018, Amazon announced a partnership with financial companies Berkshire Hathaway and JPMorgan Chase to apply technology to reduce the costs of health care while at the same time helping patients become healthier. Bezos's belief in focusing on long-term goals was apparent in his statement about the plan: "Hard as it might be, reducing healthcare's burden on the economy while improving outcomes for employees and their families would be worth the effort. Success is going to require talented experts, a beginner's mind, and a long-term orientation."[5] The health-care field is a $3 trillion industry, and it is clear that Amazon is seeking to claim its own place in it.[6]

THE MARS CONFERENCE

Amazon is secretive about specific future plans. But an event that Bezos holds each year provides insight about what he sees as important. The ideas discussed there may offer hints at what Amazon's future holds.

The conference is called MARS, which stands for machine learning, home automation, robotics, and space

Bezos is passionate about space travel, robotics, and other cutting-edge fields.

exploration. It is an invite-only event. The third annual MARS conference was held in Palm Springs, California, in March 2018. Wide varieties of brilliant guests attended MARS. They included astronauts, designers, and actors. Major figures from business also attended, including executives from car company Ford, computer chip company Intel, and speaker company Sonos. Companies in the fields of health care and robotics were also represented at the conference. There were even scientists talking about astronomy and gravity. The attendees gave presentations on innovations in science, engineering, health, and business.

Bezos is deeply involved in the whole event. His loud, distinctive laugh tells attendees he is nearby. He dresses casually, in jeans and cowboy boots. At the 2018 conference, he played table tennis against a robot. He also took the controls of a four-legged robot built by robotics company Boston Dynamics. Inside attendees' hotel rooms, an Amazon Echo played music and answered requests. Bezos talked to attendees on the last night of the conference. "I really do believe that we are on the leading edge of an incredible renaissance. I'm so optimistic about it."[7]

TOP PUBLIC US E-COMMERCE COMPANIES BY SALES, 2017[8]

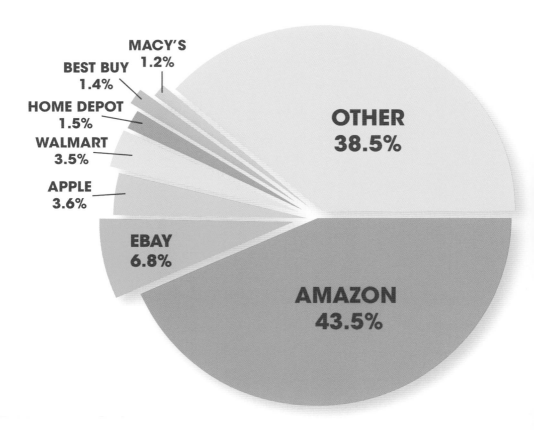

MACY'S 1.2%
BEST BUY 1.4%
HOME DEPOT 1.5%
WALMART 3.5%
APPLE 3.6%
EBAY 6.8%
OTHER 38.5%
AMAZON 43.5%

Amazon has become by far the largest public e-commerce company in the United States. It is trailed distantly by other online retailers, such as eBay, and the websites of traditional retailers such as Walmart and Home Depot.

Bezos has built a company that no one in 1994 could have imagined. It is the largest bookstore, the largest online store, and the largest cloud-services company in the world. It has a massive network of fulfillment centers and delivery systems. Amazon has changed the world, and under Bezos's leadership, it aims to continue its tradition of innovation into the future.

ON TAKING RISKS

Bezos's decision to start Amazon was a risky one at the time. He left a good job for a start-up company that might fail. In 2010, he reflected upon that 1994 decision: "It really was a difficult choice, but ultimately, I decided I had to give it a shot. I didn't think I'd regret trying and failing. And I suspected I would always be haunted by a decision to not try at all. After much consideration, I took the less safe path to follow my passion, and I'm proud of that choice."[9]

TIMELINE

1994
Jeff Bezos starts Amazon in his Seattle garage.

1995
On April 3, Amazon sells its first book; by the end of July, orders have shipped to all 50 US states and 45 countries around the world.

1997
Amazon's 1-Click ordering begins.

1998
Amazon begins to sell CDs and DVDs in addition to books.

2000
The Amazon Marketplace program begins.

2002
Amazon Web Services (AWS), Amazon's cloud computing service, is launched.

2005
Amazon introduces Amazon Prime memberships.

2006
Fulfillment by Amazon services are launched.

2007
The Amazon Kindle e-reader becomes available for purchase.

2011

Amazon's tablet, called Kindle Fire, is launched.

2012

Amazon acquires Kiva Systems in preparation for using robots in fulfillment centers.

2013

Amazon announces its plans to pursue drone delivery; Bezos buys the *Washington Post*.

2014

The Echo smart speaker is introduced, featuring Alexa as its digital assistant.

2015

Amazon opens its first physical store, Amazon Books, in Seattle.

2017

Amazon buys Whole Foods Market.

2018

Amazon Go, the first store with no checkout lines, opens in Seattle.

ESSENTIAL **FACTS**

FOUNDER AND CEO

- Jeff Bezos (from 1994)

FIRST EMPLOYEE AND ORIGINAL PROGRAMMER

- Shel Kaphan (1994–1999)

KEY STATISTICS

- On July 16, 1995, Amazon's website opened for business. By the end of the first month, Amazon had sold books to people in all 50 states and 45 countries. By December 1996, it had 180,000 customers. Less than one year later, in October 1997, it had more than one million customers.

- Amazon's nickname is the "everything store." In the United States, 40 cents of every dollar spent online is spent on Amazon.com. Amazon is now the biggest bookseller in the world.

- Amazon Web Services (AWS) is Amazon's cloud computing service. AWS provides more than 40 percent of all cloud computing services available online.

- There are more than 100 million Amazon Prime members worldwide.

- As of September 2017, Amazon had almost 542,000 workers.

- By 2018, Amazon operated 15 physical bookstores.

IMPACT ON HISTORY

Amazon was founded in July 1994 as a small online bookstore at a time when many people weren't even sure what the internet was. Amazon is now the biggest bookseller in the world and one of the largest e-commerce sites. Innovation is an important part of Amazon's success. Online customer reviews, one-click ordering, and free two-day shipping were all Amazon firsts. Amazon has also developed several successful tech devices, such as the Kindle e-reader, Fire tablet, and Echo smart speaker with digital assistant Alexa. Amazon also owns a robotics company, and founder Jeff Bezos started a private aerospace company as well.

QUOTE

"I really do believe that we are on the leading edge of an incredible renaissance. I'm so optimistic about it."

—*Jeff Bezos*

GLOSSARY

algorithm
A set of steps followed to solve a mathematical problem or to complete a computer process.

brick-and-mortar
Having a physical building where customers go to shop (as opposed to a website).

cloud computing
Using remote computing services that are accessed with the internet.

data center
A building designed to house large numbers of computers, with special attention paid to cooling systems, consistent electricity service, and network connectivity.

frugality
Being thrifty and avoiding being wasteful.

infrastructure
The basic equipment and structures that are needed for a system to function properly.

inventory
A complete list of items that a store has for sale.

publicly traded company
A company whose stock can be bought or sold by anyone.

retailer
A business that sells items directly to customers for their use.

revenue
Income, especially of a company or organization and of a substantial nature.

stock
A piece of ownership in a company. When a person buys "stock," he or she buys a little piece (called a "share") of ownership in a company.

streaming
Broadcasting live video over the internet.

ADDITIONAL **RESOURCES**

SELECTED BIBLIOGRAPHY

Brandt, Richard L. *One Click: Jeff Bezos and the Rise of Amazon.com.* Portfolio/Penguin, 2011.

Byrne, John A. *World Changers: 25 Entrepreneurs Who Changed Business as We Knew It.* Penguin, 2011.

Stone, Brad. *The Everything Store: Jeff Bezos and the Age of Amazon.* Little, Brown, 2013.

FURTHER READINGS

Eboch, M. M. *Big Data and Privacy Rights.* Abdo, 2017.

Wittekind, Erika. *Amazon.com: The Company and Its Founder.* Abdo, 2013.

ONLINE RESOURCES

Booklinks
NONFICTION NETWORK
FREE! ONLINE NONFICTION RESOURCES

To learn more about Amazon, visit abdobooklinks.com. These links are routinely monitored and updated to provide the most current information available.

MORE INFORMATION

For more information on this subject, contact or visit the following organizations:

AMAZON HQ TOURS
Seattle, WA
amazonhqtours.com

Amazon offers tours of its headquarters in Seattle, Washington, including a green office space known as the Spheres, where employees can work inside huge glass structures filled with thousands of plants.

SEATTLE TIMES
1000 Denny Way
Seattle, WA 98109
206-464-2111
seattletimes.com

The *Seattle Times* has been covering Amazon since the company's early days, and it continues to report on the tech titan's latest moves in a dedicated section of its website.

SOURCE **NOTES**

CHAPTER 1. THE RICHEST MAN IN THE WORLD

1. Elizabeth Weise. "Amazon's Jeff Bezos Was the World's Richest Man, for a While." *USA Today*, 27 July 2017, usatoday.com. Accessed 25 July 2018.

2. David Carrig. "Jeff Bezos' Wealth Is Now Equal to 2.3 Million Americans'." *USA Today*, 6 Mar. 2018. Accessed 25 July 2018.

3. "Jeff Bezos." *Forbes 2018 Billionaires List*, 2018, forbes.com. Accessed 15 Mar. 2018.

4. Laura Stevens. "Amazon's Quarterly Profit Tops $1 Billion for First Time." *Wall Street Journal*, 1 Feb. 2018, wsj.com. Accessed 25 July 2018.

5. Stevens, "Amazon's Quarterly Profit Tops $1 Billion for First Time."

CHAPTER 2. IT BEGAN WITH BOOKS

1. John A. Byrne. *World Changers: 25 Entrepreneurs Who Changed Business as We Knew It*. Penguin, 2011. 65.

2. Brad Stone. *The Everything Store: Jeff Bezos and the Age of Amazon*. Little, Brown, 2013. 64.

3. John Cook. "Meet Amazon.com's First Employee: Shel Kaphan." *GeekWire*, 14 June 2011, geekwire.com. Accessed 25 July 2018.

4. Cook, "Meet Amazon.com's First Employee."

5. Stone, *The Everything Store*, 39–40.

6. Stone, *The Everything Store*, 24.

7. Stone, *The Everything Store*, 49.

8. James Quinn. "Amazon's Jeff Bezos: With Jeremy Clarkson, We're Entering a New Golden Age of Television." *Telegraph*, 16 Aug. 2015, telegraph.co.uk. Accessed 25 July 2018.

9. Stone, *The Everything Store*, 112–113.

10. Neal Karlinsky and Jordan Stead. "How a Door Became a Desk, and a Symbol of Amazon." *Amazon Blog*, 17 Jan. 2018. blog.aboutamazon.com. Accessed 25 July 2018.

11. Byrne, *World Changers*, 70.

12. Byrne, *World Changers*, 63–64.

13. Mark Hall. "Amazon.com." *Encyclopedia Britannica*, 2018, Britannica.com. Accessed 11 Mar. 2018.

14. "Barnes & Noble Reports Fiscal 2016 Year-End Financial Results." *Business Wire*, 22 June 2016, businesswire.com. Accessed 25 July 2018.

15. Ángel González. "Amazon Sales Hit $136B in 2016; Dollar Hurts Overseas Business." *Seattle Times*, 2 Feb. 2017, seattletimes.com. Accessed 25 July 2018.

16. Byrne, *World Changers*, 64.

17. Rani Molla and Jason Del Rey. "Amazon's Epic 20-Year Run as a Public Company, Explained in Five Charts." *Recode*, 15 May 2017, recode.net. Accessed 25 July 2018.

CHAPTER 3. CHANGING BOOKS AND MEDIA

1. Mark Hall. "Amazon.com." *Encyclopedia Britannica*, 2018, Britannica.com. Accessed 11 Mar. 2018.

2. John A. Byrne. *World Changers: 25 Entrepreneurs Who Changed Business as We Knew It*. Penguin, 2011. 68.

3. Brad Stone. *The Everything Store: Jeff Bezos and the Age of Amazon*. Little, Brown, 2013. 254.

4. Ivana Kottasová. "Real Books Are Back. E-book Sales Plunge Nearly 20%." *CNN*, 27 Apr. 2017, money.cnn.com. Accessed 25 July 2018.

5. Brian Klems. "How Hugh Howey Turned His Self-Published Story 'Wool' into a Success (& a Book Deal)." *Writers Digest*, 23 Jan. 2014, writersdigest.com. Accessed 25 July 2018.

6. Klems, "How Hugh Howey Turned His Self-Published Story 'Wool' into a Success."

CHAPTER 4. INNOVATING THE SHOPPING EXPERIENCE

1. Samuel Gibbs. "Amazon Employee Rebukes Wife over Jeff Bezos Biography." *Guardian*, 6 Nov. 2013, theguardian.com. Accessed 25 July 2018.

2. Dan Frommer. "Jeff Bezos Says Amazon Has More Than 100 Million Prime Members." *Recode*, 18 Apr. 2018, recode.net. Accessed 25 July 2018.

3. "Prime Now." *Amazon*, 2018, primenow.amazon.com. Accessed 25 July 2018.

4. Darren Rowse. "11 Lessons I Learned Earning $119,725.45 from Amazon Associates Program." *ProBlogger*, 19 Aug. 2009, problogger.com. Accessed 25 July 2018.

CHAPTER 5. REINVENTING DELIVERY

1. Brad Stone. *The Everything Store: Jeff Bezos and the Age of Amazon*. Little, Brown, 2013. 73.

2. Stone, *The Everything Store*, 73.

3. Noah Robischon. "Why Amazon Is the World's Most Innovative Company of 2017." *Fast Company*, 13 Feb. 2017, fastcompany.com. Accessed 25 July 2018.

4. "See How the Holiday Rush Is a Moment to Shine." *Amazon*, 5 Apr. 2017, aboutamazon.com. Accessed 25 July 2018.

5. "Relentless.com." *Economist*, 19 June 2014, economist.com. Accessed 25 July 2018.

6. "Help Grow Your Business with Fulfillment by Amazon." *Amazon*, 2 Apr. 2018, services.amazon.com. Accessed 25 July 2018.

CHAPTER 6. RETAIL EXPERIMENTS

1. "Amazon Books." *Amazon*, 2018, amazon.com. Accessed 5 Apr. 2018.

2. Brad Stone. *The Everything Store: Jeff Bezos and the Age of Amazon*. Little, Brown, 2013. 227.

3. Sam Cinquegrani. "Analyzing Amazon's Move to Get Physical." *Ivey Business Journal*, Mar./Apr. 2017, iveybusinessjournal.com. Accessed 25 July 2018.

4. Gabriel Campanario. "Amazon Go Market's Public Opening: Long Lines In, but Getting Out Is Fast." *Seattle Times*, 22 Jan. 2018, seattletimes.com. Accessed 25 July 2018.

CHAPTER 7. AMAZON AND TECHNOLOGY

1. Steven Levy. "Amazon Is Dead Serious about Delivering Your Goodies by Drone." *Wired*, 31 Mar. 2017, wired.com. Accessed 25 July 2018.

2. Levy, "Amazon Is Dead Serious about Delivering Your Goodies by Drone."

3. Ed Oswald. "Here's Everything You Need to Know about Amazon's Drone Delivery Project, Prime Air." *Digital Trends*, 3 May 2017, digitaltrends.com. Accessed 25 July 2018.

4. Noah Robischon. "Why Amazon Is the World's Most Innovative Company of 2017." *Fast Company*, 13 Feb. 2017, fastcompany.com. Accessed 25 July 2018.

5. Robischon, "Why Amazon Is the World's Most Innovative Company of 2017."

6. "Amazon Picking Challenge." *RoboCup 2016*, 2017, robocup2016.org. Accessed 25 July 2018.

7. Ben Fox Rubin and Roger Cheng. "Fire Phone One Year Later: Why Amazon's Smartphone Flamed Out." *CNET*, 24 July 2015, cnet.com. Accessed 25 July 2018.

8. "About AWS." *Amazon*, 2018, aws.amazon.com. Accessed 17 Apr. 2018.

9. Tomas Laurinavicius. "Can Google Challenge Microsoft and Amazon for Cloud Supremacy?" *Forbes*, 10 Apr. 2017, forbes.com. Accessed 25 July 2017.

10. Larry Dignan. "All of Amazon's 2017 Operating Income Comes from AWS." *ZDNet*, 1 Feb. 2018, zdnet.com. Accessed 25 July 2018.

CHAPTER 8. CRITICISMS OF AMAZON

1. Spencer Soper. "Inside Amazon's Warehouse." *Morning Call*, 18 Sept. 2011, mcall.com. Accessed 25 July 2018.

2. Sandy Smith. "Two Worker Deaths in September at Different Amazon Warehouses Spawn Concern from Worker Advocates." *EHSToday*, 5 Oct. 2017, ehstoday.com. Accessed 25 July 2018.

3. "Amazon's Fulfillment Network." *Amazon*, 2018, aboutamazon.com. Accessed 4 Apr. 2018.

4. Soper, "Inside Amazon's Warehouse."

5. Julie Bort. "Amazon Now Employs a Whopping 542,000 People and Plans to Hire Thousands More." *Business Insider*, 26 Oct. 2017, businessinsider.com. Accessed 25 July 2018.

6. Seth Fiegerman. "The Typical Amazon Employee Makes Less Than You Think." *CNN*, 23 Apr. 2018, money.cnn.com. Accessed 25 July 2018.

7. Jodi Kantor and David Streitfeld. "Inside Amazon: Wrestling Big Ideas in a Bruising Workplace." *New York Times*, 15 Aug. 2015, nytimes.com. Accessed 25 July 2018.

8. Kantor and Streitfeld, "Inside Amazon."

9. David Streitfeld and Jodi Kantor. "Jeff Bezos and Amazon Employees Join Debate over Its Culture." *New York Times*, 17 Aug. 2015, nytimes.com. Accessed 25 July 2018.

10. Streitfeld and Kantor, "Jeff Bezos and Amazon Employees Join Debate over Its Culture."

11. Steven Pearlstein. "Is Amazon Getting Too Big?" *Washington Post*, 28 July 2017, washingtonpost.com. Accessed 25 July 2018.

12. "Amazon's Taking Another Bite of the Publishing Pie." *Authors Guild*, 8 May 2017, authorsguild.org. Accessed 25 July 2018.

13. Jim Milliot. "Publishers Are Urged to Monitor Amazon Buy Buttons." *Publishers Weekly*, 23 Mar. 2018, publishersweekly.com. Accessed 25 July 2018.

14. Alyssa Pagano and Steve Kovach. "How Amazon Gets Away with Not Paying Taxes." *Business Insider*, 26 Apr. 2018, businessinsider.com. Accessed 25 July 2018.

15. Pagano and Kovach, "How Amazon Gets Away with Not Paying Taxes."

16. Rex Nutting. "Trump Is Right: Jeff Bezos Is a Genius at Not Paying Taxes." *Market Watch*, 5 Apr. 2018, marketwatch.com. Accessed 25 July 2018.

17. Jeremy Bowman. "Trump Is Right. Amazon Is a Master of Tax Avoidance." *USA Today*, 9 Apr. 2018, usatoday.com. Accessed 25 July 2018.

18. Nutting, "Trump Is Right."

19. Colin Lecher. "What to Know about Trump's Escalating Fight with Amazon." *Verge*, 14 Apr. 2018, theverge.com. Accessed 25 July 2018.

20. Lecher, "What to Know about Trump's Escalating Fight with Amazon."

21. Youyou Zhou. "An Oregon Family's Encounter with Amazon Alexa Exposes the Privacy Problem of Smart Home Devices." *Quartz*, 25 May 2018, qz.com. Accessed 25 July 2018.

CHAPTER 9. THE FUTURE OF AMAZON

1. Matt Weinberger. "Amazon's $970 Million Purchase of Twitch Makes So Much Sense Now: It's All about the Cloud." *Business Insider*, 16 Mar. 2018, businessinsider.com. Accessed 25 July 2018.

2. Weinberger, "Amazon's $970 Million Purchase of Twitch Makes So Much Sense Now."

3. John Ballard. "Amazon.com's Twitch Is Dominating the Game Streaming Market." *Motley Fool*, 26 Nov. 2017, fool.com. Accessed 25 July 2018.

4. Kristin Houser. "Amazon Is Really Serious about Making Healthcare a Part of Its Future." *Futurism*, 26 Mar. 2018, futurism.com. Accessed 25 July 2018.

5. "Amazon, Berkshire Hathaway, and JPMorgan Chase & Co. to Partner on US Employee Healthcare." *BusinessWire*, 30 Jan. 2018, businesswire.com. Accessed 25 July 2018.

6. Dom Galeon and Christianna Reedy. "Amazon Just Opened a New Lab Dedicated to Healthcare Tech." *Futurism*, 27 July 2017, futurism.com. Accessed 25 July 2018.

7. Jackie Snow. "Jeff Bezos Gave a Sneak Peek into Amazon's Future." *MIT Technology Review*, 22 Mar. 2018, technologyreview.com. Accessed 25 July 2018.

8. Rani Molla. "Amazon Could Be Responsible for Nearly Half of US E-Commerce Sales in 2017." *Recode*, 24 Oct. 2017, recode.net. Accessed 25 July 2018.

9. John A. Byrne. *World Changers: 25 Entrepreneurs Who Changed Business as We Knew It*. Penguin, 2011. 66.

INDEX

ABOUT THE **AUTHOR**

SHANNON BAKER MOORE

Shannon Baker Moore is a freelance writer who writes for adults and children. She has lived throughout the United States, but Saint Louis, Missouri, is her current home, where she lives with her family and a pet bunny named Peaches.

ABOUT THE **CONSULTANT**

ANTHONY ROTOLO

Anthony Rotolo was a college professor for more than ten years, teaching at Syracuse University. He taught courses in technology and media, including the very first college class on social media. He is now studying for a PhD in psychology and researching how social media affects people and society.